Welcome to

SAN FRANCISCO

PACK LIST

Remember to check local weather before setting out!

DATE / /

Weather

Mood

Things I did

Food I tasted

Words I learnt

How's your day?

Is this your first time here?
Did you make new discoveries today?
Did you enjoy San Francisco's food?

Draw the things you love!

"San Francisco is the fourth-largest city in California."

Happy moments

Photo of the day #1

Photo of the day #2

DATE / /

Weather

Mood

Things I did

Food I tasted

Words I learnt

How's your day?

What do you like about San Fransico?
What's your favorite part of the day?

Draw the things you love!

Happy moments

Photo of the day #1

Photo of the day #2

DATE / /

Weather

Mood

Things I did

Food I tasted

Words I learnt

How's your day?

Do you find local people friendly and helpful?
What did you see today?

Draw the things you love!

"The Golden Gate Bridge has been a popular target for destruction in movies, such as Superman (1978) and Godzilla (2014)."

Happy moments

Photo of the day #1

Photo of the day #2

DATE / /

Weather

Mood

Things I did

Food I tasted

Words I learnt

How's your day?

Do you like where you are staying?
Who do you miss most from home?

Draw the things you love!

Happy moments

Photo of the day #1

Photo of the day #2

DATE / /

Weather

Mood

Things I did

Food I tasted

Words I learnt

How's your day?

What do you miss about the trip?
Would you want to return one day?

Draw the things you love!

"The bendy straw and denim jeans were invented in San Francisco."

Happy moments

Photo of the day #1

Photo of the day #2

Where do you want to go next?